# Angel's Task

Laurie Patton's new collection of poems, *Angel's Task*, is rooted in a deep reverence for the ordinary gestures of daily life, how our rituals of existence enact a kind of midrash—a conversation with scripture, a filling in of the gaps. In delicate, thoughtful language, the poems range from Moses pondering the stone tablets or Noah haunted by what he's left behind, to a speaker reveling in the quiet communion with God through our day-to-day recognitions: "the small square of sun / on the side / of a single olive / where the whole orchard / is reflected." What a beautiful notion Patton gives us, the illumination manifest in our own actions: "these are the lights / that hold / our backward, earthly glances / as we turn our eyes / toward heaven."

—NATASHA TRETHEWEY, author of *Bellocq's Ophelia*, and *Native Guard*, winner of the 2007 Pulitzer Prize

When Moses disobeys God and, instead of speaking, in anger he strikes a rock to get water out of it for a whining people, he loses his chance to enter the Promised Land. "The rabbis say / God wanted / Moses' words / to be the miracle," begins Chukat, a poem in Laurie Patton's marvelous new book of midrashic poems, *Angel's Task*. The poem concludes with a question: "Why do we not know / even now, / that speech is enough?" Perhaps Moses didn't trust the power of his own words, but we can feel the power of Laurie Patton's words on every page of this inquisitive, inventive, wise, and beautifully written book. Questions propel the poems, questions triggered by the short passages of Torah with which each poem begins. But you do not need to be familiar with or even interested in the Bible to be fully engaged by these poems, as the poems transport us into the lives of their various speakers—Noah, an angel, Moses, an adulterous biblical woman, and a contemporary woman offering observations, in one poem, on billboards that line the road home from an airport, to name a few. Of course, if you do study Torah, you will be amazed at how those old, familiar verses, when twisted and turned by a poet as intelligent and imaginative and skilled as Patton, will yield new insights. And while a poet will recognize and admire Patton's deft control of tone, image, and line, among other elements, any reader will find that the poems in *Angel's Task* accomplish one of poetry's most important tasks: to speak in a way that awakens a reader and enables her to see more clearly the complexities of her own heart and mind and the challenges and predicaments of our contemporary moment. That's the miracle of *Angel's Task*.

—RICHARD CHESS, author of *Tekiah, The Chair in the Desert,*
and *The Third Temple,* and former poetry editor of *Zeek:*
*A Jewish Journal of Thought and Culture*

# Angel's Task

Laurie L. Patton

**Station Hill**
of Barrytown

Published by Station Hill Press, Inc., 120 Station Hill Road, Barrytown, NY 12507, as a project of the Institute for Publishing Arts, Inc., in Barrytown, New York, a not-for-profit, tax-exempt organization [501(c)(3)], supported in part by grants from the New York State Council on the Arts, a state agency.

Online catalogue: www.stationhill.org
e-mail: publishers@stationhill.org
Interior and cover design by Susan Quasha
Cover art by Lika Tov

Library of Congress Cataloging-in-Publication Data

Patton, Laurie L., 1961-
Angel's task / Laurie L. Patton.
    p. cm.
ISBN 978-1-58177-144-2 (alk. paper)
1. Jewish religious poetry, American. I. Title.

PS3616.A9265A85 2010
811'.6—dc22

                                        2010045285

Manufactured in the United States of America

*For Arnold Goodman*
*and in memory of*
*Ozna Robkin*

# Contents

# Introduction

CAUGHT WITHIN THESE PAGES is a set of contemporary responses to Biblical verses. I write "caught" because *Angel's Task* is both structured and accidental. It is structured in that each poem is based on a weekly section, called a *parasha* (plural *parshiyyot)*, of the Torah, or five books of Moses. This form of division goes back in the Jewish tradition as early as the tenth century, and probably much earlier. *Parshiyyot* are found in a text called the Aleppo Codex, a Tiberian copy of the Torah thought to be the oldest in existence. The Aleppo Codex, in turn, is the text that the great thinker Maimonides used in writing his own work on the laws of composing the Torah scrolls.

But these dry facts do not do justice to the poetic possibilities of the *parshiyyot*. In most cases, a new *parashah* begins when there is a new thought or new subject introduced in the Torah. Each *parashah* is named by the first few words that begin the section. Thus, to take the most well-known example, *Bereshit* means "In the Beginning." When we open *Bereshit* to read, we know that the first few words, signifying beginning, will color the rest of the text. To take another example, *Bamidbar*, "In the wilderness," is the first *parashah* of the Book of Numbers. The name of this *parashah* covering Moses' deliberations with his people in the desert, and everything else occurring in that *parashah* is, in some way or another, also associated with that wilderness.

But it is not always the case that there is an easy alignment between topic and division in the Torah. There are some *parshiyyot* that may not seem like new topics, and some new topics that are not marked by a division. And in this ambiguous situation lie further poetic opportunities: each division suggests the possibility of newness, even when such newness is not necessarily clearly presented.

Jewish tradition also emphasizes a style of commentary called Midrash, from the Hebrew root *darash*, "to seek," "to study." Forms of Midrash can include prosaic explanations, parables, and legends. Midrash is designed to respond to the "gaps" within the Torah that are not fully explained or narrated in the text itself. They can take a number of shapes: a philosophical musing; an allegorical tale; a background to a narrative; a point of view of a character not told or, perhaps not even present; an elaboration of what happened after the narrative ended. Scholars believe that the traditional Midrashic commentaries were composed between 400 and 1200 CE. However, there are many contemporary writers and thinkers who argue that the Midrashic tradition continues to the present day, and that the practice of constant commentary in prose, poetry, allegory, and philosophy actually keeps the Biblical tradition alive in the contemporary world. This book comes out of that last perspective—the idea that Midrash is always possible, and a form that can engage the reader in new ways of encountering old texts.

*Angel's Task* is also the result of a contemplative practice of reading. This practice of reading assumes that in each *parashah* there is an opportunity for a poem, and that the verses that could serve as the occasion for the poem will emerge for the reader over time. It is a matter of letting the text take hold of the reader, rather than the other way around. Contemplative reading involves waiting. One waits and allows the images within the text to apprehend one's sensibilities.

This practice also assumes that there is no "single meaning" or "most important meaning" to the text; there are no verses that are more important than other verses. Rather, all verses are equally important as potential places for the poetic imagination to land. There is a Hebrew saying, "The verse, 'Lotan's sister is Timnah' (1 Chronicles 1.39) is as important as any other verse in the Torah."

This aphorism suggests that any verse, no matter how mundane, is ripe with interpretive possibilities. Although certain verses did emerge as the occasion for my own poetic Midrash, I am certain that if I started the practice again it would result in an entirely different set of poems.

Contemplative reading is, however, the opposite of the practice of "Bibliomancy," or "Bible magic," found in 19th century American Christian communities, or even the more recent idea of a "Biblical Code," where predictions and answers to common questions are provided by finding Biblical verses that "solve" the questions. Contemplative reading, in contrast, creates ambiguous connections between the Biblical text and the reader, connections which are not answers, but further questions. Contemplative reading implies that Biblical verses do somehow illuminate the stuff of everyday life in the twenty first century life—billboards on a highway, the memory of sibling rivalry, the cardboard dwelling of homeless person over the grate of a city street. Such illumination is not a static "ending" of the process of interpretation, but rather a dynamic and fluid beginning, pressing the reader on to further reading and further contemplation. While each poem is a single vision evoked by a Biblical verse, the voices the poems take on are multiple. At times, it seemed best to work in the voice of the Biblical character. At other times, it seemed best to adopt a contemporary voice. I chose whatever voice seemed the most powerful for engaging the human particularities implied by the verse.

The readings of each *parashah* represent singular poetic moments. This idea is also captured in the Jewish understanding of the angel's task, a phrase which inspires the book's title. It is well known that the Hebrew word for angel, *malach*, means "messenger." It is less well known, however, that angels are in fact beings sent to earth with a single piece of work to accomplish. For a second piece of work to be accomplished, a second angel would be necessary. In this book, I explore this idea in the poem, *Vayeira*. But the notion of the angel's task informs all of the poems; each poem fulfills a particular piece of poetic work at a particular moment in time. Like the angel, each poem performs a particular task—the result of a unique confluence of Biblical verse and everyday insight.

Laurie L. Patton,
*Atlanta, Georgia*

# Bereshit  בראשית

*And God said: "Let the waters swarm with swarms of living creatures, and let fowl fly above the earth in the open firmament of heaven." And God created the great sea-monsters, and every living creature that creeps, and with which the waters swarmed, after its kind, and every winged fowl after its kind; and God saw that it was good. And God blessed them, saying: "Be fruitful, and multiply, and fill the waters in the seas, and let fowl multiply in the earth." And there was evening and there was morning, a fifth day. And God said: "Let the earth bring forth the living creature after its kind, cattle, and creeping things, and the beast of the earth after its kind." And God made the beast of the earth after its kind, and the cattle after their kind, and every thing that creeps upon the ground after its kind, and God saw that it was good.* —GENESIS 1.20-25

Is good
the pure instinct
of owls,
whose single notes
over fences
chill the night?

Is good
the whales'
simple refusals
to hide from the boats
who track them?

Is good
the labrador
who obeys a soft voice
(but whether for love
or food is still
hotly debated)?

Is good
the taste of blood
at the throat
of a rabbit
shaken dead
in the grass?

Is good
the clean, efficient
downward glance
of the heron?

Is good
the way
I cannot imagine
any cruelty
in mountains
so green and jewel-like?

Is good
the way
You have made
all this—

Or is good
the way
we are stunned
by Your creatures,
confounded
by goodness?

# Noach  נֹחַ

*And Noah the husbandman began, and planted a vineyard. And he drank of the wine, and was drunken, and he was uncovered within his tent.* —GENESIS 9.20-21

I couldn't stop the memory;
wine was the only way,
and lying without my robe
a small price to pay
for oblivion
from the flashes:

On the boat's threshold,
wet fur is filling
my nostrils—
a stampeding,
screeching stench
of feathers and flanks
the odor more ominous
because the rain
has already started;

And they keep coming
in their swaggering stink,
each with breath
in their nostrils
as the Lord said;

And the ropes come off
and I lean over the gunwale
swaying thirty cubits high,
while inside, their hissing
and spitting drones on
with the roar of the thunder;

Then I hear the screams
of the ones left behind,
and I see them
on the shore
struggling in the trees
and flapping in the soil
and racing toward us
eyes wide, and wild, and white—
there was breath
in their nostrils, too,
as the Lord said
They are racing toward us;
and our pale outlines
are their last glimpse
of survival;

My hand grips the gunwale
and I stand frozen,
swaying thirty cubits high,
watching the steaming boil
of terrified life

And their outlines
then burn into memory
as I turn away
forever

# Lech Lecha לֶךְ לְךָ

*And [Abram] said: "Lord God, whereby shall I know that I shall inherit it? And he said to him, "Take to me a heifer of three years old, and a she-goat of three years old, and a ram of three years old, and a turtle dove, and a young pigeon." And he took him all of these, and divided them in the midst, and laid each half over against the other; but the birds he did not divide. And the birds of prey came down upon the carcasses, and Abram drove them away. And it came to pass that, when the sun was going down, a deep sleep fell upon Abram, and lo, a dread, ...even a great darkness, fell upon him.... And it came to pass... that the when the sun went down, and there was thick darkness, behold a smoking furnace, and a flaming torch that passed between these pieces. In that day the Lord made a convenant with Abram, saying, "Unto thy seed have I given this land...."*—GENESIS 15.8-13; 17-18

I had known
the pattern of pieces:
placing a ram's leg
next to the heifer's,
and the goat shank,
bursting with muscle,
over these again.

My ancestors taught
that each part
called to a god:
an ear for the god
who gives hearing,
and a tongue for the one
who grants speech;

and we could tell
from the way
the pieces fell
against each other,
what would happen
in our father's house;

But I was far
from my father's house,
and I could not hear
the talk of the gods
the way we used to,
even though I strained—

I strained so hard
I slept
from the struggle
and the despair of it;

And yet a flame woke me,
and that fire blew
between the pieces,
brought them together
one by one
like a red vein;

there was a holiness
in that fusing flame,
making one beast,
one fire,
one peace.

# Vayeira וירא

*And the Lord appeared to him by the terebinths of Mamre, as he sat in the tent door in the heat of the day; and he lifted up his eyes and looked, and three men stood over against him; and when he saw them, he ran to meet them from the tent door, and bowed down to the earth, and said, My lord, if now I have found favor in thy sight, pass not away, I pray you, from your servant.* —GENESIS 18.1-3

As angels,
we have one task,
and only one task;
we are created
for a single purpose.

So you can imagine
the odd way
Abraham and Sarah
struck us
when we arrived—
all distraction in dark winds.

Turning first to us
in servant bows;
and then rushing inside
for meal and cakes;
and then again,
to the animals—
all indecision,
haste, and trembling.

When we told the news
of her future son,
Sarah tried to hide
her soft laughter,
and there was more trembling,
while she bent her face
in the windy shadows
of the tent.

And then Abraham
wavered again
as we walked toward
Sodom and Gomorrah–
gleaming cities of waste
and black delusion;
like a fishmonger,
he tried to bargain with God
shaking all the while,
and pleading for God
to give up His anger.

We were just messengers
when we saw them,
but Abraham and Sarah
were possessed
of so many minds
and so many tasks.

So we marveled,
when our task was done,
that the two still knew
that God was with them,
even with all their trembling.

# Chayei Sarah חיי שרה

*And Isaac and Ishmael his sons buried [Abraham] in the cave of Machpelah, in the field of Ephron, the son of Zohar the Hittite, which is before Mamre...* —GENESIS 25.9

**Ishmael:**
> I was thirteen,
> and I remember the music
> and my mother whispering,
> "Why such a party, when
> it is only a weaning?"
> And the smell of lamb
> and the tambourines;
> and the involuntary sound
> coming from my own throat—
> half laughter, half-sob—
> after I saw my mother's face
> in the firelight;
> and I knew
> my little brother
> was now my rival.
> But God was still good to us—

**Isaac:**
> —and I was three,
> and I remember
> staring out in the dark
> of the morning
> and seeing two shadows

and then the clear outline
of your mother
clutching a water bottle,
and watching her wave
in the air,
as if she were talking
to Someone.
But God was still good to us—

**Ishmael:**
—and now we stare together
into the cave
that holds our father—

**Issac:**
—our father's bones and memory,
in the place before Mamre—

**Ishmael:**
—and yet I fear
for the future—

**Isaac:**
—since perhaps the only thing
we can do together

**Ishmael and Isaac:**
is to bury
and to mourn
our dead.

# Toldot תּוֹלְדוֹת

*And Jacob said to his father: "I am Esau you firstborn; I have done what you asked of me. Arise, I ask you, sit and eat of my venison, that your soul may bless me."* —GENESIS 27.19

There was a moment
of fragile wholeness
as I placed the spicy stew
in my father's shaking hands;

My thin white skin
covered in his goat-hide,
I was my brother
and he was me.

With all my years of study,
I could still drip blood.
We could both be
the hunter and the sage.
We even smelled the same.

And the fog of lies
and play of mirrors
resolved for an instant
into a clear reflection;
each brother
the image of the other—
a pattern of beauty.

Then it shattered
as I opened my mouth
to answer my father.
I knew my brother
could never be me,
nor I him.

We went on
to live out our jealousy,
stubbornly dreaming
under the quiet stars.

# Vayeitzei ויצא

*And Rachel stole the teraphim that were her father's ... Now Rachel had taken the teraphim, and put them in the saddle of the camel, and sat upon them. And Laban felt about all the tent, but found them not.*
—GENESIS 31.19; 34

I laughed
at my father's
devotion
to them.

He would peer
around the corners
of our rooms
to check on them,
as if sun and moon
were down the hall.

Now their heads
are jumbled
in the bag.
Their eyes stare blankly,
wrapped in dark cloth.

But even as they lie
helpless under my thighs,
I have not forgotten
that they once stood,
proud upon his shelf.

# Vayishlach וישלח

*...For Jacob said: I will appease him with the present that goes before me, and afterward I will see his face; perhaps he will accept me (lit. lift up my face).* —GENESIS 32.21

*And Jacob called the name of the place, "Peniel: 'For I have seen God face to face, and my life is preserved."* —GENESIS 32.31

*And Jacob said "No, I pray you, if I have found favor in your sight, then receive my present at my hand; for as much as I have seen your face, as one sees the face of God, and you were pleased with me."* —GENESIS 33.10

**Jacob to Esau:**
There were so many faces
on my path yesterday:
your soldiers,
my wives and children,
anxiously pacing
opposite sides
of the river.

I thought of praying,
and sending ewes and rams,
donkeys and foals,
and yes, I would have fought you.

Instead, I saw not you,
but a man full of light
gripping my thigh.

In laughter? In anger?
I could not tell.
He showed his face
but refused his name.

Then you came,
full of light,
like the man.
Like him,
you had a face
that could have,
but did not,
destroy me.

And now we fall
on each other's necks.
We have escaped
the fate
of the first brothers.

I do not yet trust you,
but am content
to feel
your pulse in my hands.

# Vayeishev וישב

*And the [brothers] took Joseph's coat, and killed a he-goat, and dipped the coat in the blood; and they sent the coat of many colors, and they brought it to their father; and said: "We have found this. You might know now whether this is your son's coat or not. And he knew it, and said: "It is my son's coat: an evil beast has devoured him; Joseph is without torn in pieces." And Jacob rent his garments, and put sackcloth upon his loins and mourned for his son many days. —*GENESIS *37.31-34*

When I made the coat,
I imagined shades
of his mother.
The blues, greens, and grays
were colors of her eyes
at different times of day.

The coat could wrap him
and give him blessings,
as she did.
She had light songs
on her breath for him
until she no longer
walked with us
on earth.

And when I saw the coat
shredded in blood,
and I imagined him
also in pieces,
I began to tear
my own clothes.

Stitch by even stitch
I undid them.
Each tear
a promise to myself:

Never again will I
create things of beauty—
never again
wrap my love
in something other
than exhausted prayer.

# Mikeitz מקץ

*And [Joseph's brothers] said to one another: "We are truly guilty*
*concerning our brother; for we saw the distress of his soul when he beseeched*
*us, and we would not hear; therefore this present distress has come upon*
*us." And Reuben answered them, saying, "Did I not say to you, 'Do*
*not sin against the child, and yet you would not hear? So, see now, that*
*his blood is required." And they did not know that Joseph understood*
*them; for the interpreter was between them. And [Joseph] turned himself*
*around, away from them, and wept... —Genesis 42.21-24*

    I remember now.

    My disguise
    was arrogance

    In answer,
    you threw me down,
    shouting, "We are not brothers."

    I became
    a slave—
    another face,
    among the spices
    and balm and ladanum
    in the wagons
    bound for Egypt.

Now I have
another disguise—
Egyptian in tenor:
Zapenath Paneah,
"Keeper of the Mysteries."

Your words of regrets
ring sharply
by my silos of corn.

I could throw you down.
Keep you as slaves
to hunger and remorse.

But, as Keeper
of the Mysteries,
I keep my disguise
for a little longer,
so that I may weep.

# Vayigash ויגש

*...all the souls of the house of Jacob that came into Egypt were threescore and ten. And [Jacob] sent Judah before him to Joseph, to show the way before him to Goshen; and they came into the land of Goshen. And Joseph made ready his chariot, and went up to meet Israel his father, to Goshen, and he presented himself to him and fell on his neck, and wept on his neck a good while. And Israel said to Joseph: "Now let me die, since I have seen your face, that you are yet alive." —GENESIS 46.27-31*

My sons showed me
the way to Goshen,
where I would set up
a house of teaching.

What would be taught?

I feared that Joseph
would not be there,
and I would only
learn again
the Talmud of loss,
where each letter
was chiseled out
by the grief
of a century,
and in each equation
there was an empty space
for my son.

But I was wrong.
The equations were filled in.
My house of teaching
included a resolution
of the numbers:
"eleven"
no longer meant
"twelve minus one."

Such lessons
for my thinning heart
left me heavy,
and smiling,
hanging on Joseph's neck.

# Vayechi ויחי

*And Joseph took an oath of the children of Israel, saying, remember you,*
*and you shall carry up my bones from hence. So Joseph died, being a*
*hundred and ten years old. And they embalmed him, and he was put in*
*a coffin in Egypt.* —GENESIS 50.25-26

Uncle Sid bought the plot
for himself and Aunt Louise,
and kept the deed
in a mahogany case
for fifty years;

And famous explorers
lie with their family
tucked in white marble,
solid as Mars.

Our bones don't move.
We can hardly imagine them
in the ground,
never mind
dug up again,
lifted by a loving hand
toward the place
we *should* be buried.

How could Joseph imagine,
even at the moment
of his death,
that he would not rest,
even then?

What final dream
Is this to interpret—
this dream of bones
clattering toward Zion?

# Shemot שמות

*And the child grew, and she brought him to the Pharaoh's daughter,
and he became her son. And she called his name "Moses," and said:
"Because I drew him out of the water." (*min ha maim m'shitihu.)
—EXODUS 2.10

What if our names
were not just reminders
of our bodies,
snapshots of flesh
and color—
*John Smith at ten,*
*holding the dog;*
*John Smith at seventeen,*
*with girlfriend?*

What if our names
were remembrances
of the places
where our souls
were drawn out
into the world?

John–*gift from God,*
Smith–*the great metalworker:*

So we might say:
*the great metalworker*
*who comes from God*
*at ten, holding the dog;*

or

*the great metalworker*
*who comes from God*
*at seventeen,*
*with girlfriend.*

Then John Smith
is always
bringing forth iron
from the earth
in God's presence.

Then Moses is
is always
being plucked
by God
from the muddy wavelets.

What if a name
was a memory
of that first struggle
when three shapes—
wet body,
wet earth,
and God—
were becoming one?

# Va'eira   וארא

*And the Lord spoke to Moses and to Aaron, saying, "When Pharaoh
shall speak to you, saying: 'Show a wonder for you,' then you shall say to
Aaron, 'Take your rod, and cast it down before Pharaoh, that it becomes
a serpent.' And Moses and Aaron went in to Pharaoh, and they did
as the Lord commanded, and Aaron cast down his rod before Pharaoh
and before his servants, and it became a serpent. Then Pharaoh also
called for the wise man and the sorcerers; and they also, the magicians
of Egypt, did in like manner with their secret arts. For they cast down
every man his rod, and they became serpents; but Aaron's rod swallowed
up their rods. And Pharaoh's heart was hardened, and he hearkened
not to them, as the Lord had spoken.* —EXODUS 7.8-13

It's not unusual, really,
to feel the heat
of Pharaoh's breath,
our patrons wheezing
behind us,
with admiration
and cudgels.

And we, the magicians,
frantically wonder
how to make snakes:

snakes who crawl
the doorposts in August,
green predictions
of fertility;
snakes who encircle
the physician's staff,
with smooth promises
of healing;
snakes mistaken
for twisting ropes–
our philosophers' examples
of false perception.

How do we know
we are not simply
failed magicians
weaving arrogant spells
in weakness?

How do we know
we are not always battling
a superior magic?

# Bo בא

*And they shall eat the flesh in that night, roast with fire, and
unleavened bread; with bitter herbs they shall eat it. Eat not of it raw,
nor sodden at all with water, but roast it with fire; its head with its legs
and with the innards thereof. And you shall let nothing of it remain
until the morning; but that which remains of it until the morning you
shall burn with fire. And thus you shall eat it: with your loins girded,
your shoes on your feet, and your staff in your hand, and you shall eat it
in haste—it is the Lord's Passover. —Exodus 12.8-11*

"Chew slowly!" our mothers said
in old kitchens with tiled floors
where we drew a map,
trying to find a country
for those shadowy starving children
whom we neglected in our haste.

"Fast food" is a necessary sin:
the lettuce dropped
on the dashboard
for the next driver to note;
the hiccup endured
throughout the day
because we ate too much
while walking,
the exhaust from the buses
blowing over our bread
like so many spices.

But somewhere,
there could be a man,
chained to his digits and data,
the patterns
of computed numbers
bouncing off the threads
of his suit.

That man might tear off
the wrapping from the daily special,
and gulp it down,
because he knows
that when he walks outside
on his quiet gray carpet,
his chin dripping
with low-calorie oil,
he will see the doorposts
of his corner office
marked in red,

and he will know
that God will be waiting
on the other side.

# Beshalach בשלח

*But the children of Israel walked upon dry land in the midst of the sea; and the waters were a wall unto them on their right hand, and on their left. Thus the Lord saved Israel that day out of the hand of the Egyptians, and the people feared the Lord; and they believed in the Lord, and in His servant Moses. Then sang Moses and the children of Israel this song unto the Lord, and spoke, saying,*

> *"I will sing unto the Lord, for He is highly exalted;*
> *The horse and his rider hath He thrown into the sea."*
> —EXODUS 14.29-15.1

Why do we always sing at the sea?

Is it the waves,
who pull the moon
and our hearts
like beats on a drum?

Is it the surf,
that old percussion
reminding us
that people once fished
under pink cliffs
in hard canoes?

Is it the gulls
whose voices trail off
in appealing wails,
so that their cries
and the children's,
bouncing after balls,
become, for a moment,
the same?

Or is it
that we remember
something else,
even older,
and almost forgotten:
the crash of freedom
in a curling wave,
the crush of a soul
imprisoned by water?

Why do we always sing at the sea?

# Yitro  יתרו

*And all the people saw the thunder and the lightning, and the voice of the horn, and the mountain smoking; and when the people saw it, they trembled, and stood afar off. And they said to Moses, "You speak with us, and we will hear; but let not God speak with us, lest we die." And Moses said to the people, "Do not fear, for God has come to prove you, and that his fear may be before you, that you do no evil. And the people stood afar off, but Moses drew near to the thick darkness where God was.*
—EXODUS 20.15-18

When I spoke
with the people of Israel,
they saw thunder.
Perhaps it was only
the fine vibrations
of the air.

Or perhaps they saw
the colors of sounds,
like the finest of poets.

They knew
that they could not come
any closer to the Presence,
and pushed me
up the burning mountain,
like younger brothers
push their elders
on afternoon treasure hunts.

Finest of ironies:
I had just reassured them
that I would go,
and would not die!
And so, too, did God
reassure me.

And yet now
that I am stumbling
up these craggy footholds
toward His rumbling smoke,
how do I know
that I will live?

Perhaps it is because
I have died
so many smaller deaths,
my stiff neck bent,
my doubts burned clean
by that Voice.

There is nothing in me
left to consume.
I am free to be
the first to fall
into His holy fire.

# Mishpatim מִשְׁפָּטִים

*And if you at all take a neighbor's garment to pledge, you shall restore it to him by that the sun goes down, for that is his only covering; it is his garment for his skin, wherein shall he sleep? And it shall come to pass, when he cries to me, that I will hear, for I am gracious.* —EXODUS 22.25-27

We've always known
that clothing makes a world;
tents on our mother's beds,
earth and sky made of quilts
letting the light in
so that we are small makers
of tiny suns and miniature moons,
each requiring new stories.

We've always known
that our shawls
are second skins,
which, unlike snakes,
we have the blissful choice
of removing at will.

We've always known
that blankets
have an inch of heat
that can be the difference
between life and death
for someone newly nameless
searching for a subway vent.

We make
tiny worlds,
and shed skins,
and seek warm winds:
in these ways
we cry to You,
and You hear,
because You are gracious.

# Terumah תרומה

*And let them make me a sanctuary, that I may dwell among them.*
—EXODUS 25.8

Ben Jacob wrote:

> On Sinai,
> God dwells in a sanctuary
> which His hands have made;
> now he is to dwell
> in a sanctuary
> which Israel would make,
> and the Tabernacle would be
> a wandering Sinai.
>
> In the desert,
> we always imagine,
> and then hammer
> beam, post, and ring
> with new hands and fingers
> in mind:
> what will corners be like
> for knuckles barely bending
> and fingers over-bent?
>
> How much more so
> for God, the new arrival–
> so used to His own home
> in Sinai,
> but now come to dwell with us.

Of His reasons,
we are not sure,
but we are still planing,
surfacing, and smelting.

We know
he made Leviathan
with them,
but for carpenters,
it is still hard
to imagine
God's hands.

How will they
touch the walls
as He turns the corners?

# Tetzaveh תצוה

*And you shall put the whole upon the hands of Aaron, and upon the hands of his sons, and shall wave them for a wave-offering before the Lord. And you shall take them from their hands, and make them smoke on the altar upon the burnt offering, for a sweet savor before the Lord; it is an offering made by fire unto the Lord.* —EXODUS 29.24-25

> God's knowledge
> is from the ancient brain.
>
> When we walk outside
> after a storm,
> and sniff wet leaves
> mixed with onions
> from the kitchen down the street,
> we think of something
> wider than ourselves.
>
> The smell of book binding,
> birdseed, and fruit
> in our grandmother's room
> propels us
> toward her arms.
>
> Burnt toast
> in the morning,
> acrid and welcoming,
> causes our blood
> to rush toward the sun.

Surely these are
sweet savors before the Lord.

# Ki Thissa    כי תשא

*And it came to pass as soon as he came near to the camp, that he saw the calf and the dancing; and Moses' anger waxed hot, and he cast the tables out of his hand, and he broke them beneath the mount.* —Exodus 32.19

*And the Lord said to Moses, "Carve for yourself two tablets of stone like the first, and I will write upon the tables the words that were on the first tablets which you broke. And be ready, by the morning, and come up in the morning to Mt. Sinai, and present yourself there to me on top of the mount. And no man shall come up with you, neither let any man be seen throughout all the mount, neither let the flocks nor herds feed before that mount. And he hewed two tables of stone like the first, and Moses rose early in the morning, and went up to Mt. Sinai, as the Lord had commanded him, and took in his hand two tablets of stone.* —Exodus 34.1-4

> The first time
> I stumbled
> down the mountain
> with the stones,
> their letters
> were like diamonds—
> gifts I did not comprehend.
>
> I finally arrived,
> breathless and squinting
> into the valley.

But it wasn't the stones
that made it hard to see
their twisted dancing;
the statue had blinded me
with its gold flashes.

I roared at the dancers then.
I tried to stop the noise.
The stones split open
on the ground.

Now, alone and quiet,
I make the stones again.
Every edge is smoothed
by sweat and breath.
I carve, hammer, and rub down
by the light of the stars.

Now, pieces of stone
fall again
around my feet.
Chiseled,
not shattered.

I am thinking
of the letters
that will come again
in the morning–
an alphabet healed,
a broken stroke made whole.

How could I break them again?

# Vayakhel וַיַּקְהֵל

*Moses then called together the whole Israelite community and said to them: These are the things that the Lord has commanded to do: On six days may work be done, but on the seventh day you shall have a sabbath of complete rest, holy to the Lord; whoever does any work on the sabbath day shall be put to death.* —EXODUS 35.1-2

The rabbis
rushed to say
that we don't really die
if we work on Shabbat.
They were sure
that the second soul,
who arrives
on that day,
dies instead.

What does
a second soul
look like?
Not a grey,
gentle, man
who comes to the door
with a sad smile,
and leaves
just as politely,
in a whisper
through the fog.

No.
My second soul
is crouching now
under my chair,
a panting animal
for whom breath,
and rest, and sun
are the same.

Such a creature
does not go lightly,
but dances
to every tune
offered up
by the wind.

# Pekudei פְּקוּדֵי

*When Moses had finished the work, the cloud covered the Tent of Meeting, and the Presence of the Lord filled the Tabernacle. Moses could not enter the Tent of Meeting, because the cloud had settled upon it and the Presence of the Lord filled the Tabernacle. When the cloud lifted from the Tabernacle, the Israelites would set out, on their various journeys; but if the cloud did not lift, they would not set out until such time as it did lift. For over the Tabernacle a cloud of the Lord rested by day, and fire would appear in it by night, in the view of all the house of Israel throughout their journeys.* —EXODUS 40.34-38

The first night,
jolted from sleep,
I thought there had been
an accident, or a fire.

Perhaps it was
the first fire
in the bush,
encircled by sheep
in the shaking air;
so I sat up, dumbfounded.

Perhaps it was
the fires
of our huts in Egypt
smoldering
as we left them;
so I rose to flee.

Perhaps it was
the hissing sparks
of the smith's hammer,
pounding the last jewels
in the golden calf;
so I raised my arms
in anger.

Then I saw
the fire
was in the Dwelling Place,
settled and glowing,
like in the best of houses;
so I breathed slowly
back to sleep.

# Vayikra ויקרא

*For you shall burn no leaven or honey as a burnt-offering to God ... they shall not ascend the altar for a fragrant odor.* —LEVITICUS 2.11

Perhaps they knew
this was not the honey
stored patiently in glasses
by clear-eyed, solemn, keepers;

not the honey
placed on each letter
of the Hebrew alphabet
by doting masters;

but a wilder liquid
congealing in the corpse
of a lion
waiting for Samson
to dip his hand
in a hungry rage;

the oozing honeycomb
that interrupts
a restful woodland
cell after packed cell
threatening decay.

Perhaps they knew
such untamed sweetness
might resist
the fires of God.

# Tzav צַו

*And Moses took the anointing oil, and anointed the tabernacle and all that was therein, and sanctified them. And he sprinkled thereof upon the altar seven times, and anointed the altar and all its vessels, and the laver and its base, to sanctify them. And he poured the anointing oil upon Aaron's head, and anointed him, to sanctify him.* —LEVITICUS 8.10-12

This was no sprinkling.

It was more majestic,
and thorough.
The desert world
stood solemn
as Aaron's whole head
was oiled;
and then it gleamed,
pink and comforting,
while the sand and stone
cooled in the evening.

But however dignified
Aaron was that day,
he must also have thought
of a child's bath,
and a woman's hands
tracing white rivers of soap
down his head.

At once priest and infant,
he must have known
the strong, safe palms
of a mother,
and of Moses,
and of God
had become one.

# Shemini שְׁמִינִי

*You shall not make yourselves detestable with any swarming thing that swarms; neither shall you make yourselves unclean with them, that you should be defiled thereby. For I am the Lord your God; sanctify yourselves therefore, and be holy; for I am holy; neither shall you defile yourselves with any manner of swarming thing that moves upon the earth.*
—Leviticus 11.43-44

In Durban, we saw
a swarm of brown locusts.
Their wings wove
a thousand webs,
humming invitations
from the blue
to expand forever.

It was a single whole—
seamless and lovely.
And we stared.
When it broke apart
into single beings,
we swatted at our legs
in mute panic.

Then it shot back up
into the sky
as a single whole,
and we stopped,
and stared again.

It could have danced
that way forever.

When I was ten,
I decided that our bodies
were just a swarm of cells.
We looked like single wholes,
then we broke apart
into so many creatures:
sperms, germs, cancers.
Later we battled
to become whole again.

A swarm
is the struggle
between singular and plural
the in-between state
that horrifies.


It forces us to kneel down
in the sand,
close our eyes,
and declare things holy.
Holy,
or at least clear,
now and forever.

# Tazria  תזריע

*And the garment, or the warp, or the woof, or whatsoever thing of skin
it is, which you shall wash, if the plague is departed from it, then it
shall be washed a second time, and shall be clean. This is the law of the
plague of leprosy in a garment of wool or linen, or in the warp, or in the
woof, or in anything of skin, to pronounce it clean, or to pronounce it
unclean.* —LEVITICUS 13.58-59

It takes time
to clean
and wrap
leprous bandages.

Elijah told the rabbi
that the Messiah
was a leper
sitting at the gates
of the city,
bandaging his wounds
one at a time.

"Ah," said the rabbi,
"he is being thorough.
He is taking his time."

"No," said Elijah.
This way,
he can come
any time
that he is called,
and he will not be delayed."

Such a Messiah
would rush out—
no time for cover
or cleaning:

What is one open sore
when the moment has come
to close the wounds
of the world?

# Metzora מצרע

*He shall examine the mark [to determine if] the mark on the wall of the house consists of penetrating streaks that are bright green or bright red, which appear to be below [the surface of] the wall. [If they are,] the priest shall leave the house [and stand just outside] the entrance of the house. The priest shall then quarantine the house for seven days. On the seventh day, he shall return and examine [it to determine] whether or not the mark has expanded on the wall of the house. —LEVITICUS 14.37-39*

Something there is
that *loves* a wall:

the twilight sounds
between beam and plaster;
the ghost of damp feet,
dropped seed,
and shredded twig.

I listen
when the moon
cannot comfort.

While they build nests,
I speak to them
in the dark.
They answer, rustling.

Their messages
are authorless,
like the heart-shaped stain
on the ceiling,
or the music
in the water pipe.

It is better
not to specify them
as *genus,* or *species,*
*furry,* or *scaled.*

Something there is
that *loves* a wall,
and the subject
of that sentence
shall remain open—

as open
as their caverns
of delight.

# Acharei Mot אַחֲרֵי מוֹת

*And Aaron shall lay both of his hands upon the head of the live goat, and confess over him all the iniquities of the children of Israel, and all their transgressions, even all their sins, and he shall put them upon the head of the goat, and shall send him away by the hand of an appointed man into the wilderness.* —LEVITICUS 16.21

The "appointed man"
is *ish iti*;
the rabbis say he is
"a man outside of time,"
walking with all our sins
into a swathe
of beetles and branches–
no past, no present, no future.

*Are sins outside of time?*
Consider the stain
on my great-great-
grandmother's tablecloth.
It congealed in a moment.
I don't know
whose moment it was.

No one got divorced then.
Before the decree,
Mr. Grandmother was jailed
for disorderly conduct.
She walked with a limp.

The stain I see
every sweet Sabbath
is the same
as the sadness
still falling
from her picture,

like some stray
warning light
from the street
that awakes us
from an uneasy dream.

# Kedoshim קדשים

*Turn ye not unto the ghosts, nor unto familiar spirits; seek them not out, to be defiled by them: I am the LORD your God.* —LEVITICUS 19.31

My ghosts are not
the forbidden kind:

not the muscle twitches
we mistake for taps
on the shoulder,
nor the settling planks
we swear
are feet on the stair.

Not the familiar spirits—
the lost grandmothers
who come to our dreams
(one of mine
lounges in her chaise,
and waves in the breeze;
the other
holds a washcloth,
and waits for something
to clean.)

My ghosts are more recent:
the pillow shifting back
to its full shape
after your head
has left it;
the coffee grinds
on the tiles, telling
the morning movement
of your hands;
the yawn from your room
still echoing, even after
you have gone to sleep.

Poor Saul,
hungry and defeated,
went in secret
to the woman of Endor;

but love has me go
openly, every day,
to the place of conjuring.

# Emor אֱמֹר

*Command the children of Israel, that they bring unto you pure olive oil beaten for the light, to cause a lamp to burn continually. Without the veil of testimony, in the tent of meeting, shall Aaron order it from evening to morning before the Lord continually; it shall be a statute forever throughout your generations.* —LEVITICUS 24.1-3

Imagine the different lights
pouring into the oil:

The one on the face
of the oil presser
as the sweat
comes down
in rivulets
and falls in one drop
from his chin

the small square of sun
on the side
of a single olive
where the whole orchard
is reflected

the pale sheen
on the stones
of the oil press,
which, while at rest,
look like old palms
turned up
to the sky

the gleam
in the eye
of the farmer's son
as he ignores
his father's calls
and stays with
his lover
for one more hour,
under the oldest tree
in the longest row—

these are
the smaller eternities
swirling through
the priestly oil

these are the lights
that hold
our backward,
earthy glances
as we turn our eyes
toward heaven

# Behar  בהר

*And the land shall not be sold in perpetuity; for the land is Mine, for ye are strangers and settlers with Me."*—LEVITICUS 25.23

"All the beaches should be free!"
she would say,
while she left
her latest dark dream
on the kitchen counter
behind her,
and walked
toward the sea weed
and the snails—
the next homes
to welcome her.

"All the beaches should be free!"
she would say,
while she spread
her arms wide,
in hope of gathering up
the waves and clouds together,
like the first pillows
to be thrown
into an empty, waiting room.

"All the beaches should be free!"
she would say,
and she would speak to me
of possible worlds
that vanquish noonday demons—
where fishes govern
in harmony
with ospreys,
and bankers and sailors
cast an equal vote
with seals.

"Perhaps you are right,"
I would say;
perhaps there is a better cure
in the cool democracy
of a shoreline;
in the acceptance
of driftwood
and the open chorus
of far away voices,
playing over
the welcoming strand.

# Bechukotai בחקתי

*The sound of a driven leaf shall chase them; and they shall flee, as one flees from the sword; and they shall flee when none pursues.* —LEVITICUS 26.36

Of course
a driven leaf
shouldn't frighten.

A skeleton
of spring,
it skates on surfaces,
an oat-colored reminder
of hope
(or perhaps,
the loss of hope).

But it does not rattle us
awake in the night;
it does not grasp our shoulders
in menacing surprise.

But wait:
there are those
small whirlwinds
at dawn,
known only
by the circular path
of the leaves
rising upward,

as if they were tracing a person
who stands before us,
and yet refuses to appear.

This is terror:

the outline of a presence
calling to us,
whom we can never hold

the rasping leaves
telling us
as the sun rises
that our longing
that will never be sated—

not by dawn,
not by a quieted storm,
not by a hand,
no matter how strong.

# Bamidbar במדבר

*And the Lord spoke to Moses in the wilderness of Sinai, in the tent of meeting, on the first day of the second month, in the second year after they had come out of the land of Egypt, saying: "Take the census of all the congregation of the children of Israel, by their families...*
—NUMBERS 1.1-2

*(Census of all the congregation of the children of Israel: "seu et rosh kol adat benei yisrael."—lit. "the lifting up of the head")*

Once, counting was
a possibility—
counting when lying down
on Stage Island,
where the grains of sand
were theoretically possible
to number;

we could also imagine
an end to the blades
of blue crab grass
sweeping from the house
into Bobby Sears' brown barn

The kind of finitude
that thrilled
and sickened
because its boundaries
had huge and mysterious
lines—like the oceans of beaches
and the fences of neighbors

And if we started to count,
which would we remember?
the word theoretically?
or the word possible?

But perhaps counting
might also mean
another kind of end:
the lifting of the head
after blushing,
or after finishing
the last page
of a book,
or when daring, at last,
to answer—

perhaps God
meant a counting
that ended with a face—
a counting
less theoretical—
and less possible—
but when finished,
the first dazzling hint
of infinity

# Naso  נשא

*...If a man's wife has gone astray and broken faith with him...*
*and there is no witness against her...or if a fit of jealousy comes over*
*him and he is wrought up about his wife although she has not defiled*
*herself...Then the man shall bring his wife unto the priest, and shall*
*bring her offering for her; the tenth part of an ephah of barley meal; he*
*shall pour no oil upon it, nor put frankincense upon it; for it is a meal*
*offering of jealousy, a meal offering in remembrance of wrongdoing.*
*And the priest shall bring her near, and set her before the Lord. The*
*priest shall take sacral water in an earthen vessel and, taking some of*
*the earth that is on the floor of the Tabernacle, the priest shall put it*
*into the water... The priests shall adjure the woman, saying to her, "If*
*no man has lain with you, if you have not gone astray in defilement*
*while married to your husband, be immune to harm from this water*
*of bitterness that induces the spell. But if you have gone astray while*
*married to your husband..., may the Lord make you a curse and an*
*imprecation among your people, as the Lord causes your thigh to sag*
*and your belly to distend... And the woman shall say, "Amen, Amen!"*
—Numbers 5.12-17; 19-22

The priest has brought me near.
I am set before the Lord.
You stand by, watching.

His arms
are outstretched,
as they always are
when he comes
to the altar.

But the barley
does not shine
with oil,
nor is the smell
of spices upon it.

"Drink," he says.

He asks me
if I taste bitterness.

And I ask you:

How will the barley
be sour
if I remember
only the sweetness
of the bread
you placed on my tongue?

How can this water
churn my insides
if I call to mind
the wine
circling the rims
of our cups
as our fingers touched?

My spell of memory
is stronger
than any mud
he could make me drink:

the memory of you
before this offering
came between us.

# Behaalotecha בהעלתך

*We remember the fish, which we used to eat in Egypt for nothing; the cucumbers, the melons, and the leeks, and the onions, and the garlic, but now our soul is dried away, there is nothing at all. We have nothing but this manna to look to.* —Numbers 11.5-6

Herodotus, too,
said it was easy
to remember the fish,
piled high in buckets,
with no one in Egypt
to claim them

And Jeremiah would know
the green cucumbers
since they grew
around the idols—
those scarecrows in the field
he so despised

Leeks and melons
must have been served
to Joseph
when Potiphar's wife
caressed his tingling
and half-willing arm

And David's beard,
like Aaron's, dripping with oil,
might have had scents
of onion and garlic
mashed with royal pestles
only minutes before

Such delicacies
of the tongue
came before the desert,
and came after it, too—

Foods come and go—
in whims that play
over centuries

Why then did we think
our very souls
depended on such juices
to stop their thirst
when You were waiting
at the end of our desires—

partly Subtle,
like the scent of spices
and partly Angry,
like the sound
of the beating wings
of quail?

# Shelach שלח

*And [the scouts] told Moses, and said: "We came into the land where*
*you sent us, and surely it flows with milk and honey; and this is the fruit*
*of it. But the people that dwell in the land are fierce, and the cities are*
*fortified, and very great; and also, we saw the children of Anak there....*
*and we were in our own sight as grasshoppers, and so we were in their*
*sight.* —NUMBERS *13.27-28, 33*

When one visits a Vision,
one must always
struggle with scale:

Their visit
was like watching
the shoes and skirts
and deep voices
at a parents' reception—
watching, overwhelmed
and hiding, under the stair

or the coding
and decoding
of the signals of elm trees
and broken twigs—
the ciphers of sparrows
and their forgotten eggs
in the immense forests
of an aunt's small garden

or the daily memory
of a schoolyard
filled with light—
wet, and covered with apples—
a huge space,
with windows beckoning
to the soul

Visions are so wide,
they require the courage
of painters, trying out
a new and startling scale;
and they require an answer
to the question:
*Shall I belong here?*

# Korach  קרח

*Korach said to them: You take too much upon you, since all the congregation are holy every one of of them, and the Lord is among them; why do you lift yourselves up above the assembly of the Lord?" And when Moses heard [Korach's words], he fell upon his face. And he spoke to Korach and to all his company, saying: "In the morning, the Lord will show who are His, and who is holy, and will cause him to come near unto Him.... —*NUMBERS 16.3-5

Moses gave Korach one night.

The origins of insomnia
must be in those hours,
as each man wondered
about the lands
of milk and honey,
and his rights
to hoist banners
for the crowds who loved him.

Moses sure of God's voice,
and Korach sure of his own—
each trying to tell
the difference
between arrogance
and righteous anger—
a line so thin—
thin as a flame
in a fire pan.

Their sleepless night
is our own,
echoing restlessly
as we sort spices
in our dark kitchens
and arrange furniture
by moonlight.

Sweating in starlight,
we remember arrogance
and mutter righteous anger,
and then quietly beg
to hear God—

for when the dawn comes,
we do not know
which of our sacrifices
will be holy.

# Chukat חֻקַּת

*And the Lord spoke to Moses, saying, "Take the rod, and assemble the
congregation, you and your brother Aaron, and speak to the rock before
their eyes, so that it gives forth its water"... And Moses took the rod
from before the Lord, as He commanded him. And Moses and Aaron
gathered the assembly together before the rock, and he said to them,
"Hear now, rebels, are we to bring you forth water out of this rock?"
And Moses lifted up his hand, and smote the rock with his rod twice,
and the water came forth abundantly, and the congregation drank,
and their cattle. And the Lord said to Moses and Aaron, "Because you
did not believe in Me, to sanctify Me in the eyes of the children of Israel,
therefore you will not bring this assembly into the land which I have
given them." —*NUMBERS 20.8-12

The rabbis say
God wanted
Moses' words
to be the miracle.

We forget
that speaking to rocks
is enough,
though our conversations
with them
are so very old:

the stones
thundering to Jonah
from the shores
of Nineveh,
welcoming him
from the red bowels
of the fish;

the mossy rocks
that whispered
small lullabies
in our midnight escape
from the sadness
in Egypt;

the Wall
calling out to us
with prayers
like furled kites
inside.

Why do we not know
even now,
that speech is enough?

# Balak בלק

*And the ass saw the angel of the Lord, and she lay down under Balaam;*
*and Balaam's anger was kindled, and he struck the ass with his staff.*
*And the Lord opened the mouth of the ass, and she said unto Balaam:*
*"What have I done to you, that you have struck me these three times?"*
*And Balaam said to the ass: "Because you have mocked me; would that*
*I had a sword in my hand, for by now I would have killed you..." Then*
*the Lord opened the eyes of Balaam, and he saw the angel of the Lord*
*standing the way, with his sword dawn in his hand; and he bowed his*
*head, and fell on his face.* —Numbers 22.27-31

> At eleven forty five
> in the dark,
> the dog whose eyes
> are so fixed and steady
> that I am daily convinced
> of his next, human life
>
> walked to the bottom shelf
> of the back library,
> and slowly pulled
> at a small book
> with his teeth—
> Ted Hughes,
> "Poetry in the Making,"
> the chapter on writing
> about animals.

With his paws,
he held down page fourteen,
"The Thought Fox":
a poem about a fox
who suddenly climbs
into the poet's head
at midnight.

I read between his paws:

*Till with the sudden sharp hot stink of fox*
*It enters the dark hole of the head*
*The window is starless still; the clock ticks,*
*The page is printed.*

And the dog looked up
amidst the snowy crumbs
of chewed paper

and that curtain—
that frustrating scrim
between animals like me
and the ones like him—
was lifted
in our startled gaze

"Yes, you are
the thought fox!"
I said to him,
"and yes, it is time
for you to be
inside my head!"

"And by the way,"
I went on,
"What other angels
have you been
falling in front of…

And what else
do I need to know
from their presence
in my road?"

He kept chewing
but did not answer.

# Pinchas    פינחס

*And the Lord said to Moses, "Get up to this mountain of Abarim,*
*and behold the land which I have given unto the children of Israel.*
*And when you have seen it, you also will be gathered to your people,*
*as Aaron your brother was gathered; because you rebelled against*
*My commandment in the wilderness of Zin, in the strife of the*
*congregation, to sanctify Me at the waters before their eyes... And Moses*
*spoke to the Lord, saying, "Let the Lord, the God of the spirits of all flesh,*
*set a man over the congregation, who may go out before them, and who*
*may come in before them, and who may lead them out, and who may*
*bring then in; that the congregation of the Lord are not as sheep who*
*have no shepherd." —*NUMBERS 27.12-17

If I had been
on the mountain
of Abarim
and looked down
on those jewel-valleys
imagined for so long—
the hope of every
exhausted morning—
and I had heard
God's judgement
as I stared,

I would have thrashed
and rolled on the ground
yelled about meeting goals
and productive use of time
and wasting resources.

I would have lectured God
on the philosophers'
idea of hell:
to behold the food
one desires most
and never be able
to devour it
I would be weeping still.

But I have never
attended at a birth
where the soul
must submit
to the instrument
and the labor
never goes as planned.

No one speaks
of their own longing
when the child slips,
gasping, into the air
and into reality.

How much more so
the midwifery of Moses,
who never saw the birth,
but only asked
that someone follow
so that labor
could continue.

# Mattot מטות

*Also when a woman makes a vow to the Lord, and binds herself by a bond, being in her father's house, in her youth, and her father hears her vow, or her bond, with which she has bound her soul, and her father holds his peace with her, then all her vows shall stand, and every bond with which she has bound her soul shall stand. —NUMBERS 30.4-5*

Not exactly vows,
our announcements
at the kitchen table
near the blue thistle china—
but recited with fervor.
And they did bind our souls.

"Papa, I read a poem today..."

In the mornings,
we tried
to draw his gaze
from *The Times*
by dropping crumbs
between the lines
of newsprint.

In the evenings,
we thought we might
weave ourselves
into the geometry
of the grey headlines
by plucking at his fingers
and pushing at his toes:

Ours was no ancient house
of Israel.
We moved freely
through French doors,
sucked on lemons
in cool summers,
and thumbed forbidden pages
in the hush of the library.

Yet we would have given
our starring roles
and all our poems
if only
he would turn his head

to listen, weigh,
—even judge—
our anxious words.

# Massei מַסְעֵי

*And the Lord spoke unto Moses in the plains of Moab by the Jordan at Jericho, saying, "Command the children of Israel, that they give to the Levites of the inheritance of their possession cities to dwell in; and open land round about the cities you shall also give to the Levites. And they shall have the cities to dwell in; and their open land shall be for their cattle, and for their substance, and for all their beasts..." "Speak to the children of Israel and say to them: When you pass over the Jordan into the land of Canaan, then you shall appoint cities to be cities of refuge for you, that the manslayer who kills any person in error might flee there." —NUMBERS 35.1-3; 10-11*

On the road
from the airport
squinting beyond
the air freshener

we see looming
such bright promises
of refuge—
of quick resurrections
after accidental deaths
of the soul.

Billboards mingle
in friendly chorus
with water tanks
and fire stations
and radio towers:

"No Fault Divorce?
Call Alison Wilson!"
"The Gentleman's Club:
Couples Welcome!"
"Don't Wait for the Hearse
to Take You to Church!"

Such are our city walls—
our portals of entry
into a protection
too vast to be true—

while the last open land
with cows still grazing
quietly makes
a sturdier promise:
of rain, and dirt,
and sheets,
half blown
from the laundry line.

# Dvarim דברים

*And I spoke to you at that time, saying, "I am not able to bear you myself alone; the Lord your God hath multiplied you, and behold, you are this day as the stars of heaven for multitude. The Lord, the God of your fathers, make you a thousand times so many more as you are, and bless you, as He has promised you! How can I myself alone bear your weight, and your burden, and you strife? Get wise men from each of your tribes-men who are understanding and full of knowledge, and I will make them heads over you. —*DEUTERONOMY 1.9-14

One almost thinks
of Moses
as some ancient hero,
a huge basket
of stars on his head.

Is he
like sweating Sisyphus,
carrying his burden
up Mount Horeb
with no end in sight?

Or like Atlas
with the globe
of longing and dreaming
on his shoulders?

But for Atlas or Sisyphus
to be like Moses,
they would have had
to split their boulders
like ruined tablets,
because Moses knew
the value of fragments.

Perhaps he even knew
the calcium of our bones
was formed in a star,
and each of us
had to be spread out
like so many shattered
pieces of light.

Moses also knew
he had to put
his stars down,
and arrange them
in rows,
and strange galaxies
called *Israel*.

# Va'etchanan  ואתחנן

*Take therefore good heed unto yourselves, for you saw no manner of form on the day that the Lord spoke to you in Horeb out of the midst of the fire—lest you deal corruptly, and make a graven image, even the form of any figure, the likeness of male or female... and lest you lift up your eyes to heaven, and when you see the sun and the moon and the stars, even all the host of heaven, you might be drawn away and worship them, and serve them, which the Lord your God has allotted to all the people under the whole heaven. But the Lord has taken you and brought you forth out of an iron furnace, out of Egypt, to be to him a people of inheritance, as you are this day.* —DEUTERONOMY 4.15-16; 19-20

The ancient word
for magician
is "one who can touch
the moon with his finger—"
or perhaps even snatch it
from the sky—

As God said,
the moon does rule
over the night:
it was the measure
of our backyards
when our legs
could carry us
only that far;

And it held rabbit's ears
and shone gray light
while we imagined
far away lands: London,
Latvia, Lucknow;

It dragged oceans,
unnoticed, and shone
when we first bled;

And it was the herald
of our first sips of wine
and a helpful sign
for those who staggered;

And it played rough
with out hearts
while we promised,
like in all the old epics,
to take and slice it
like sweet apples
for our lovers;

Who wouldn't long
to inherit the moon?

If we were magicians,
we would catch it
and put it in a chest,
or freeze it for flavor,
like a fat shiny fish,
and then forget
its Source.

We would desert the One
who made the lesser light—
that Fashioner
who whispered creation
as only the first
among so many wonders

# Eikev עֵקֶב

There is a lightness
when we cross a threshold—
wood-frames sunk into soft soil,
steel-frames of old tenements
that have carried the weight
of slow, sad steps above them;
sometimes, even,
a mezuzah points upward
like a finger:

No matter the sorrow,
every door holds a hope
of difference, of newness—
the thought that
our days will multiply

And then:
anticipation splinters
into the past
of a room,
where
we have to come to terms
with objects—

Take, for instance, the kitchen:
the way my eye catches
the light on the grapes,
like the boat-shells
gathered in your hands
at that lowest of tides;

or the way the bowls tilt,
like the heads of the seals
who watched us, clapping,
on Barnacle Rock;

or the way the rims
of the wine-glasses
curve, like the ripples
off your paddle
dipping near Seaweed Island;

In this doorway,
pieces of the summer
before you died
multiply like so many days
of a future—

a past hauled up
from the Zero
of forgetting
into the More-than-One
of surprised memory.

Yes,
says the red and peeling paint
of the cheerful frame:

Our days will multiply,
and they do so
in both directions.

# Re'eh ראה

*At the end of every seven years you shall make a release.*
—DEUTERONOMY 15.1

There is a sad fatigue
to the number seven:

It's the winding down
of our long march,
the end of our delight
in the stability of three
and the roundness of four;
it even lacks the nest-like
qualities of six,
where two three's
are intertwined.

We tire
when we think
of Ezekiel's seven angels
ranging over the earth
without ceasing;

our eyes close
when we are told
of the walls of Jericho
falling on the seventh day,
their stones too weak
to withstand
the holy winds;

our heads fall
as we learn
of the Romans,
finishing their city
on that seventh hill,
exhausted.

We say,
*On the seventh day, God rested.*
But perhaps we should say
*On the seventh day, God got tired.*

Perhaps seven
gives us permission
to let the wind take us,
away from all our fields,
all our cities,
and all the old, anxious
works of our hands.

# Shoftim שׁפְטִים

*And if you say in your heart, "How shall we know the word which the Lord has not spoken? When a prophet speaks not in the name of the Lord, if the thing follows not, nor comes to pass, that is the thing which the Lord has not spoken; the prophet has spoken it presumptuously, and you shall not be afraid of him.* —DEUTERONOMY 18.21-22

We know only time
can tell us the difference
between the true
and the false
lips of prophets:

*If it comes to pass—*

if the dust and fire
and choking cities
in their dreadful poems
are our own.

But then,
the prophet's job
would be easy
if all it took
was simple prediction,
like the four-year old
learning to read
the gray, moulting sky
and pronouncing, "Rain!"

Or the simple command
made of the buried,
insignificant seed,
pronouncing, "Grow!"

Or the quiet statement
of the basic facts
of decay:
of stone roads,
of steel armies,
of the heart,
and of the soul.

Yes, all these predictions
were shouted darkly
by grimy men
at the city gates.

But prophets were
not these men:

Jeremiah,
sweating and exiled,
or Jonah, stinking
and glowering
under the vine,
did not just embrace
the dust and the dark.
No.
They were furious
and impatient for God.

They could see
the ways in which
seed and heart
both quickened
to the same light—

And they wanted
that light
to crash into souls
before
the inevitable,
sad darkening.

# Ki Teitzei  כי תצא

*When you reap your harvest in the field, and have forgotten a sheaf in the field, you shall not go back to fetch it; it shall be for the stranger, for the fatherless, and for the widow that the Lord your God may bless you in all the work of your hands.* —DEUTERONOMY 24.19

What would be
the impossible occasion
of forgetting
to till a field?

Did the farmer
somehow not reckon
on that last acre,
like the inside button
in an old sweater,
or the last safety pin
on the dark top
of a bureau,
or the coins
careening wildly
at the bottom
of one's purse?

Yet I myself
never leave the house
only once,
but several times:

First I forget
that crucial book;
then that paper
with phone numbers
arranged in colored ink
like some ancient code;
then the blue umbrella
with five spokes bent;

they are all forgotten
until I force myself
to make footpaths
back and forth
between the driveway
and the kitchen door—
in little parabolas
of memory

But perhaps,
like the farmer,
I should give all
the forgotten things
away—

After all,
the phone numbers
become beloved voices;
the book's pages
hold the trance of ideas;
and the umbrella
is a small arc of heaven—

And voices, trances,
and arcs of heaven
are things
to be shared—

Perhaps God's law
is that generosity
begins with forgetting,
and is only possible
in stages.

# Ki Tavo  כִּי תָבוֹא

*You shall build the altar of the Lord your God of unhewn stones, and you shall offer burnt-offerings thereon unto the Lord thy God. And you shall sacrifice peace-offerings, and shall eat there; and you shall rejoice before the Lord thy God.* —DEUTERONOMY 27.6-7

For the wanderers,
smoke and stone
had always held
the sadness of endings:

the grey gasps
of oil wicks
as the bowls
were taken up
from the slab
that had become
their table—

or the last,
twirling breaths
of a fire
smothered by rocks
in the camp—

or the gloomy trail
in the gravel,
lit by a lamp
whose owner
stood alone
outside the tent.

Now the wanderers knew
that the smoke
hovering over them
and the stone between their hands
was no longer
an ending,
but a beginning:

the hazy birth
of their understanding
of God's lethal light.

# Nitzavim נצבים

*For this commandment which I command you this day, it is not too hard for you, neither is it far off. It is not in heaven, that you should say: "Who shall go up for us to heaven, and bring it to us, and make us hear it, that we may do it? Neither is it beyond the sea, that you should say: "Who shall go over the sea for us, and bring it to us, and make us hear it, that we may do it?" But the word is very near to you, in your mouth, and in your heart, that you may do it.* —Deuteronomy 30.11-14

Of course we would want
to go to the ends
of the sea
reaching all the while:

We would pass bright buoys
with tails stretching down
for the lobster-traps,
like the fishermens' arms
who set them;

We would pass bremen whales,
swimming wisely
between Ahab's lunging spears,
whose throats are too small
to swallow Jonah,
but whose tails
reach up to the clouds
and leave green, silent footprints
in the suddenly quiet surf;

we would squint
at the horizon
where the sun melts,
and dares us to scoop it up
like we reach for ice cream
puddling on a city street;

and we would dive down
where the ocean is heavy,
bearing the pressure
of seven tons per square inch,
extending our hands
to the last, grim seaweed
that grows without light;

We would stretch
because we are hungry fishermen
and hunted whales
and painters of the sun
and divers in the dark.

You know this is
our natural movement
toward Your word.

# Vayelech וילך

*Then my anger shall be kindled against them in that day, and I will forsake them, and I will hide My face from them...*
—DEUTERONOMY 31.17

But there are so many
kinds of hiding:

There was, for instance,
Auntie Alice, with her palm
over her eyes,
and us squealing
between the benches—

There was the small turn
of her cheek
by the elm tree
etching out
the colors of desire—

There was her face
by the city chapel
hidden by grief
and oncoming traffic,
the color of mahogany,
and dignified, too—

When hiding
has so many shades,
how will we know
that You are angry?

How will we know
we have forgotten You
and left You
like some crushed wing
fluttering on a stem
after a storm?

# Haazinu האזינו

*As an eagle that stirs up her nest, hovering over her young, spreads abroad her wings, and takes them, bears them on her pinions.*
*The Lord alone did lead him, and there was no strange god with Him.*
—DEUTERONOMY 32.11-12

A morning as usual:
steam and coffee,
and occasional glances
out the window
to the hanging begonia

where small globes
of brown feathers
were consuming moths,
minute by minute,
anxiously given,
and anxiously received;

Then an explosion
of cheerful brown fury
crashed down
on the chairs, on the sill:
and struggling wings
crossed from tile to railing—
the distance of a mountain;

And then:
from railing, to branch,
to sky, all of them—

even the elders
did not stay behind;
they, too, flew into the green,
behind the swaying winglets,
all of them gone soaring
with no strange gods
nearby

An empty nest
is deeply empty:
no proud squeals,
no turns of feathered heads
back to the begonia,
no sorrow,
no end of sorrow,
no other gods

# V'zot HaBerachah וזאת הברכה

*And Moses went up to the plains of Moab up to Mount Nebo, to the top of Pisgah, that is overlooked against Jericho. And the Lord showed him all the land, even Gilead as far as Dan, and all Naphtali, and the land of Ephraim and Manasseh, and all the land of Judah as far as the hinder sea; and the South, and the Plain, even the valley of Jericho the city of palm trees as far as Zoar. And the Lord said unto him: "This is the land which I swore unto Abraham, unto Isaac, and unto Jacob, saying 'I will give it to your seed;' I have caused you to see it with your eyes, but you shall not go there."* —DEUTERONOMY 34.1-4

Most, if they're lucky,
see their pasts
at that moment:
the truck driver
who remembers
his mother's dress
before the crash;

the bitter old man
reciting wrongs
and fingering his sheets
while the Buddhist monk
tries to tell him
between the bedpans
his life was worth something;

the matriarch, wondering,
between memories
of sledding victories
over her brother,
whether she had been
a good grandmother
after all;

No past for Moses
at death,
but only a future—
the dreamlike view
from Moab,
and the certainty
that he would lie
in an unmarked grave
while his children
farmed the quiet rows
beyond him;

his body
must disappear—
without blood,
without flashes
of memory,
and only a kiss
for a beacon
to show the way.

# Acknowledgements

For Biblical translations, I have used *The Pentateuch and Haftorahs : Hebrew text, English translation and commentary*. Edited by J.H. Hertz. 2nd ed. London : Soncino Press, 1960. I have changed language where it seemed appropriate for better English reading.

Versions of these poems have been published in the following venues:

"The Origins of Insomnia," in *Schuylkill Valley Journal of the Arts* (Fall, 2008).

"The Width of Vision," in *CCAR Journal* (Fall, 2008).

"Drawn Out" in *Studio One*, St. John's University Journal of the Arts, Vol. 33 (2008), p.49.

"Swarm" in *Red Wheelbarrow* (Spring, 2008).

"Second Soul," in *"Pheobe: A Journal of Gender and Culture* (Summer, 2008).

"Chayei Sarah"; "T'rumah"; "Tzav"; "M'tzora"; "Acharei Mot"; "Naso"; "Korach"; "Balak"; "Eikev"; in *The Torah: A Women's Commentary,* Tamara Cohn Eskenazi and Andrea Weiss, Editors. (New York: United Reform Judaism Press, 2008), pp.132; 471; 613; 676; 699; 841; 890; 913; 958; 1114.

"Noah" in *Confluence*, Volume 17 (Ohio Valley Literary Group, 2006). p. 86.

"Noah," in *Fox Cry Review* Volume XXXII (Fox Valley: University of Wisconsin, ,2006), p. 46.

"Inherit the Moon," "Census," and "Kitchen Doorpost," in *Nimrod International Journal 50.2* (Tulsa: University of Oklahoma, Spring/Summer, 2007), pp.219, 221, 223.

"Kitchen Doorpost," in *Nassau Poetry Review* Volume 9.2
(Garden City, New York: Nassau Community College,
2006), p.113

"Doorpost" in *CALYX, A Journal of Art and Literature by Women* Volume 24:1

(Corvalis, OR: Calyx Press, Summer 2007), pp 32.

"Lech Lecha" in *Kerem: A Journal of Jewish Arts* Volume 10
(Washington DC: Jewish Study Center Press, 2005-2006),
p.3.

I would also like to thank the Goldwasser Fund, Center for Creativity and the Arts, Emory University for their generous support of this project.

Several readers have lent invaluable insight: Angelika Bammer, Amy Benson Brown, Peter Berg, Michael Berger, David Blumenthal, Rick Chess, Marshall Duke, Sara Duke, Daveed Ehrlich, Sue Elwell, Tamara Eskenazi, David Finkelstein, Shlomit Finkelstein, Leila Gal-Berner, Ruth Calderon, Elizabeth Gallu, Paul Griffiths, Arnold Goodman, Michal Govrin, Eloise Halley, Leslie Harris, Susan Henry Crowe, Lynne Huffer, Miriam Karp, Herb Karp, Hazel Karp, Naamah Kelman, Mel Konner, Ruby Lal, Gilah Langner, Lauren Lapidus, Linda Lippitt, Deborah Lipstadt, Rosemary McGee, Gordon Newby, Deborah Numark, Ozna Robkin, Betsy Rosenberg, Sam Schatten, Noach Shapiro, Leslie Taylor, Natasha Trethewey, Roy Tzohar, Luke Whitmore, Ofra Yeglin. I have also had the opportunity to read and receive feedback from: The Melton Class at the Atlanta Jewish Community Center; The Temple, The Wexner Study Group, The Atlanta Chavurah.

Shalom Goldman remains best reader and first love.

# About the Author

LAURIE L. PATTON is author or editor of nine books on religion, mythology, and literature. Her most recent book of poems is *Fire's Goal: Poems from the Hindu Year,* which was named a Publisher's Weekly Pick of the Month in 2003. She has also translated the *Bhagavad Gita* for the Penguin Press Classics Series (2008). She has been the recipient of fellowships from the National Endowment of the Humanities, the American Council of Learned Societies, the Fulbright Foundation in Israel, the Fulbright Foundation in India, and the Goldwasser Fund for Religion and the Arts. She currently serves as Charles Howard Candler Professor of Religions at Emory University.